Juchitan Medusa

Alan Catlin

Červená Barva Press
Somerville, MA

Červená Barva Press
P.O. Box 440357
Somerville, MA 02144-3222

www.cervenabarvapress.com

Bookstore: www.thelostbookshelf.com

Cover Photography: Susanna Lewis

Cover Design: William J. Kelle

Production: Jonathan Penton

ISBN: 978-1-950063-72-7

Contents

Juchitan Medusa

Juchitan Medusa

Once, she may have been
Nuestra Senora de las Iguanas,
our lady of the iguanas,
her hat a turban of reptilian
heads and bodies dried to a
grotesque parody of a living
creature and fashioned as a hat
worn on carnival days. Her face
painted the palest of white
to enhance the Medusa effect;
all men who do not stop to
pick her up along the side
of the road where she waits
in her low cut silk gown hand
sewn orchids and desert flowers
forever in unnatural bloom,
are turned to the hardest
of stones. Now, she is a painted
woman of the night, her scornful,
drink addled face, an animated piece
of a Diego Rivera hallucination,
a swirling wall mural of the three
stages of life and death framed
in the hollowed craters of the painted
death head: the marriage bed beneath
a frame blessed painting of our lord,
the hospital beds beneath the our lady
of mercy cross and the R.I.P headstone
waiting for the final descent of this
woman, propped up on the cafe table
by the inertia of the alcohol
inside her, the last puffs of her
hand rolled cigarette waiting to be
inhaled, the ashes from the spent
ones coating the drained shot glasses
before her on the table, urns
for the dead and what comes after.

Premira Comunion

The marriage in white is not
with the body of Christ but
the celebration of a union between
a child and the angel of death.
Her flowers are a bouquet of white
roses to be scattered in the grave
with each shovel full of rich
dark earth. The mask that conceals
her eager face is a death head
haloed by a growth of dark,
finely combed hair, a head hand-
carved-from-wood and painted
a garish white, although now,
it is smudged and gray from prolonged
wear and abuse, unlike the candy ones
from la fiesta dias, that are so soon
devoured and disposed of, long before
the costuming days are over
and the dance bands are compelled to stop.

Rosario, Cristina and Liza

"Be it life or death, what we crave is reality."
H.D. Thoreau

Who knows how old they are
in days and years, the pale cast
of an imminent death already
painted on their old-in-their-teens
faces, dark lip glossing an
enhancement of features made cold
by a lifetime spent in street wars
as companions to East LA Warlords
and their soldiers. Liza's black
Murder Ones do not conceal her
aggressive, haughty disdain for all
things not of her own hood nor do
Rosario's seductive eyes reveal
the truth of her sensuous nature.
Her right hand is posed in a provocative,
sexually suggestive manner, long pointed
fingernails the kind that get under
the skin and leave permanent wounds
but it is Cristina who is the acknowledged
leader of this pack soon-to-be-dead
angels, her fierce eyes and lips pursed,
contorted, expressive of an uncontainable
rage, that desire to be perceived as
numero uno in this world, her index
finger extended gesturing in such a way
that is meant to be not only definitive
but obscene.

Pablo Neruda's Fight Club

are the liberators, generals
in the people's army,
memorialized as statues
and in a massive book,
Canto General, hundreds
of pages of heroics, according
to Pablo, for whom liberty
was paramount, political
oppression a kind of death
for the poet of the common man,
put down like an animal,
or so his driver said.
Pinochet was his Tyler Durden,
whose fight club spawned
death squads who came for
marked men and women at
night and made them gone,
disappeared, into walls,
new building foundations,
for gymnasiums for boxers and
indoor ranges for pistol practice,
automatic weapon fire.
Even now, the sound of
supercharged, front end modified,
Ford Falcons inspire mortal
dread, the kind of fear that
forever alters dreams.

Faux Self-Portrait of the Artist as Spanish Dancer

"I see you with a rose in your teeth,
one more thin gypsy thief"
                    L. Cohen

"Nothing makes a woman look so old as desperately
trying to look young."
                    Coco Chanel

All the poems she ever dreamed,
duende stolen from the lips of gypsy
lovers, she imagines a blood wedding for,
are the essence she tries to impress,
in costume, as a randy dancer, on spider
web sites she pretends to be someone
else for, wishing for a celebration she
could dance at, in black tango clothes,
thigh high cut in the front to reveal legs
defined by murderous hours of modern
dance, classes she audits for the dress
rehearsal rags they play, so she can sing
along with suicide lyrics, or face the firing
squad with someone else's body,
no blindfold necessary. Not even
blooms pinned to her surgically removed
chest, are ruffled by bullets or insults,
nor the flowers pinned to her hair.
Nothing can reclaim the beauty of her
youth, so remote now, you'd think her life
was photo shopped for effect, as if
false images could remove all the years
time's acid has etched into her, mostly-
hidden face, though try, she will, despite
what the mirror tells her about letting go.

Teatro di Morte

"It was the season of rain and death"
                    Wm. Faulkner

Soot collects on the rims of glasses
the old men clutch between arthritic
hands, wrinkled skin, liver spotted,
mottled, unhealthy as specimens
spilled from collection jars, staining
preserving liquids remain on the wood
long after they dry in a near-dark
barroom, spider webbed and old roof leak
musty, the air inside oppressive as
an embalming room kept sealed as
evidence that something happened here
and might one day be investigated.
All as quiet here as a lab after
the experiment has failed and all
the patients, control groups, have died,
sitting up where they were placed and
photographed for pictures at an exhibition
for some future undetermined time,
when new drinks will be poured and handed
out as party favors and life would somehow
go on as if nothing happened here to
interrupt the flow.

El Jefe

His portrait suggests a man accustomed
to always having his smallest orders,
trivial whims, carried out to the fullest
extent without question or hesitation.
Even in the jungle, his uniform would be
perfectly pressed, totally stain free,
and his boots spit polished by orderlies
whose lives would depend upon his appearance.
Ray Bans conceal the exact coloration
of his eyes, and are meant to suggest
inscrutability and manliness, but reveal
his truer, inner, animal nature: cunning
without intelligence, strength without
honor. His moustache is his vanity,
trimmed precisely and as necessary to his
face as his uniform is to his body.
What he sees, staring straight ahead is
unknowable, through the hint of a smirk
suggests he is thinking of his latest
senorita, la concubine, waiting at the spare-no-
expense luxury apartment he has secured for her,
rather than what he is seeing immediately
outside the frame. Not long after he is deposed,
his name no longer inspires awe. If he is
remembered at all it is for the two most
notable acts of his term in office:
the calling out of the National Guard
to settle a close call in a football match
with blood and dispersing a crowd at a
bull fight for booing the announcement
of his daughter's name, then randomly choosing
men from the crowd as they were leaving,
lining them up against the nearest wall,
and watching, as they are summarily shot,
the way he would be, without comment.

A Day in the Life of the Disappeared, Argentina

Waking up is with one eye looking toward
the window to make sure there are no bars.
After breakfast, you hear them arrive in
force, three military trucks heavily armed
just for you and your husband. Escape
is impossible but you try anyway and
they beat you for it later, not that they
wouldn't have beaten you anyway.
Your husband was still asleep when they arrived
but he may be dead and buried standing up in
a wall in Argentina. What becomes of the child,
rapt with wonder, not understanding why mommy
is taking a low wire fence, at a single bound,
tripping and falling, her face a smear of blood,
her front teeth cracked, as they take her
into a truck and start the motors again.
It may be months, or years, perhaps a lifetime,
before anyone understands exactly what happened
to the disappeared lying face down in a truck,
hands cuffed behind her back, she thought
that the torture began in the camps but
she was wrong. Knowing she is defenseless,
pregnant, and a political prisoner, they began
the shock treatments jolting her stomach,
her genitals, her brain, hoping to stimulate
a spontaneous abortion, not to hear
what she might have to say about the revolution,
but to listen to her scream.

In Cases of Suspected Emigration by Large Groups of People Who Could be Family Call This Government Sponsored Number

You spend all of your life locked
in a cell that knows no respect for
the sexes, for humanity, knowing only
that you are to be bound day and night
across the eyes. Seeing is prohibited
once you disappear, you must remain
invisible, and be made to act accordingly,
even though you may cry out in pain.
All the radios inside the school have been
turned up so loud, all you hear is the
bass trembling inside the walls, but you
know from experience, what they are
trying to conceal. Some nights the lights
dim periodically, making sleep impossible,
knowing someone is strapped to an electrified
metal bed spring that sends points of pain
past endurance through the body.
Even after you've talked, they send a jolt
or two through the nerve endings as a reminder
next time, if there is one, it will probably
be worse. Sometimes, when they are torturing,
and the radios are especially loud, news breaks
through, and then everything stops. Once we
heard a government broadcast that gave a
number we should call whenever we saw large
groups of people who could be family
emigrating by bus or by rail. I wondered
how many of the poor of my people were
detained here and disappeared on the way
to a funeral of a beloved relative or on the way
to a wedding feast that never took place.

The Grandmother of the Disappeared, Nicaragua

There are no words to describe
her eyes, set in casts of stone,
and sealed shut with grieving for
the child reared in her lap who is now
lost forever. In the cup of her hands
is his face, the image the family
showed all around town, door to door
asking: "Have you seen this man
and, if you have, where and when,
we implore you." No one had seen
him dragged behind the death squad
car, chained to the back bumper,
already beaten beyond belief,
proving it doesn't pay to disagree
with what is written in red paint
on all the walls of a life hemmed in
by machine guns and warlords who
collect human ears in a black
steamer trunk. After the war
they will be freeze dried and
displayed and two of them will be his.
"If he's gone, we'd like to
give the body a proper place to rest.
Just a hint, a phrase, a clue,
nothing definite, we'll never tell."
"There is nothing to tell." Her kinsman
say and to look at her, you know that
they are right.

The Family of the Disappeared, Nicaragua

I see him first, the son, entering
his teens, wondering when it will happen,
what day will it be that I too
will become nothing. Playing at war
with guns is no game. You can see
the war in his mother's eyes, already
tired beyond her years, sensing
the broken bone yards he will have
to cross in order to survive adolescence.
It is the road her husband was struck
down on, in the prime of life, speaking out
in a time where silence prevails.
It is the silent nights she holds in her
hands, nights she remembers the touch
of his flesh, so long ago removed and
made unreal, that makes her a widow
years before the fact. Her mother completes
the family portrait, staring away from
the camera as if fearing the lens
will steal her soul from her body,
completing the wasting away of her
existence, as it removed her man, long ago
on a night like this, when it was dark
and still and all you could hear
was the engines of a secret police.

General Cemetery, Santiago, Chile

The wall in the graveyard has three
grooves cut into concrete at the top
on which three death heads have been
cut from stone. The light in the
picture makes each of the journeys
up the passage to death a dark one
ending in a primitive face except for
the left one which has been blown away
as if to be buried here, even death
is not sacred; that all who came to be
here have suffered an eternal misfortune.
Looking at the heads that remain in this
general cemetery, this place that claims
all those that say what should never be
vocalized, we feel the pain of the head
removed, the unclaimed that live, or
having died a violent death, have been
made unknowable. They are nothing now
and can be remembered only at the point
of their death, in agony, or resigned,
facing a firing squad. There is only this
to know, the graves' end head is eternal,
in a place such as this, where the spirit
is weak.

Funeral for the Victims of Security Force, Santiago, Chile

There is a dead man in the velvet lined
coffin that should be the center of the picture,
except the man who took it, chose to represent
only a corner of the victim's life. Rather,
it is the living that fascinates him. And
The child, who is barely ten years old,
and terribly out of focus; a confused young
person in black, staring, uncomprehending
over the casket into the wreathes, the flash
of the camera that defines her life on a day
of mourning that marks her forever on the list
of security forces to come; you can see it in
her eyes, the future: an incomprehensible,
violent death, black flowers, everywhere
she will go and that place where she will
end, if she is lucky, as the one to be buried here.

Outside the Morgue, Santiago, Chile

The young man appears to be sleeping
in a black and white photograph
of the rest of his life. Above him
are two hard wood coffins strapped
to the vehicle his family rides
to and from markets, to and from
funerals, this double deck tandem rack
confirms: this is not the first time
we have buried two, perhaps, the last time
it was four or one. What difference
does it make? This is a family used
to grieving: the dead are on the roof
and they are dancing on his dreams.
When he awakes, he will have to dig
their graves, throw dirt in their faces,
but even underground, he will never
forget their dancing, will never
dream again without them.

Guards National Stadium, Santiago, Chile

Who knows what they are doing here,
armed as if for the next world war behind
the wrought iron fence, tips spiked to prevent
incursion, or to prevent the peasants from
interrupting what? Regular flights off the runways?
the service men from moving freely on the
tarmac? What riots are these National
Guardsmen trying to prevent with their
metal helmets and modern rifles on line
for shooting whatever it is they see on
the other side of the fence? It is the officer,
the generalissimo in the soft hat, that
disturbs. He, who is smoking an unfiltered
cigarette, his white arm band rumpled at his
left elbow, his pistol holder unsnapped.
He is in command without a doubt, and whatever
it is he is seeing beyond those dark aviator
sunglasses, is in for big time trouble;
what they do is execute, some things are
timeless, some things transcend Chile,
transcend the photograph or the poem,
and they are the victims of what will
happen next, off-stage, the unrecorded fact.

Detainee Refugee Camp, USA

He looks as if he were born
to spend his life in a yard surrounded
by fifteen-foot-high concrete walls,
topped with rolls of barbed wire,
and buttressed by guard towers.
He looks like Harry Houdini on
a five-day drunk waking up on
Riker's Island, freshly tattooed
with iguanas on each arm and death
head skulls on each side of his chest.
"Mia madre con amor" it says, in script,
between the talking heads and the devil
looking up from his navel as if amused,
holding a trident that pokes the hull
of a ship whose mast and crew have
seen better days and much troubled water.
The man whose body contains all this woe,
bears an expression that suggests:
I can break these bonds, I can slip
free from these handcuffs, I can,
if only I knew how.

Detainees Playing Soccer, USA

The field has been wet for a long
time but no one cares who plays here.
They are refugees, undesirable anywhere,
allowed out only for recreation
in a fenced-in yard.
Going toward the end line, is the half
back, alone in the frame, except for
a gaunt, tattooed man, eating paint in protest
of the living conditions, as he stands
against the white washed barracks walls
that line up next to the dismal field.
The kick downfield is an unfortunate one,
the trajectory low and weak as if
the kicker had been shot in mid motion,
on purpose and perhaps he had been,
out of focus, trying to escape.

The Room in Which the Detainees' Belongings Are Stored

What they owned hangs on meat hooks,
in canvas bags, from the ceiling like
sides of beef. Inside each bag, is a
short story, that begins in poverty and
ends in the grave. The room is so
antiseptic it feels like a morgue,
it feels as if you are imagining someone's
funeral, years before it will begin.
There is such an air of permanence about
all this worthless clothing, you can
never imagine anything in here
without a tag on its toe telling
the date of death. What the photo says,
beyond that, is that you can emigrate
to America and are disappeared, if you don't
believe it could happen, here are their possessions,
which may never be reclaimed.

Detainees' Bathroom/Solitary Confinement, USA

The wet rot is evident in the eyes
of the attendant holding the human
detritus in the collapsed circles of
his eyes. In his folded arms are
the ragged towels the condemned use
to dry themselves off with after
they have showered in the steam pits
of hell. The bathroom stalls show
where the waste leaks between floors
and forms puddles at the feet of the people
who use them. Wet tissues stick to
the walls in rolls and in sheets,
people unroll and write their future in shit
and leave them in bowls for others to flush.
It seems inhuman to imagine people living
like this but in solitary there is nothing
but a metal toilet and a window
amidst cinder blocks admitting light
for the photograph, that becomes the poem
after that, hard walls to scream at,
a bed no one could ever sleep on,
a blacking out that does things to the brain.

Pablo Neruda on Isla Negra After the Fact

Amidst the rubble, the keening
widows dressed entirely in black,
shadows cast against the white washed
walls, a frieze of pain frozen
to wail.
Amidst the accumulation of a lifetime,
pictures torn from frames punctured
and soiled underfoot, drenched
in the blood of tropic birds, animal
feces, the dung of the ages spread
as seed over potteries and statuettes
cast aside and broken as verses are
by gunfire and by pain.
Amidst the mythic sea creatures unleashed
dreaming the unwritten words that lie as
heavy as copper pennies on the dead poet's
eyes, he lies in white face, black gloves
on the pale crossed hands covering
the hollow cave of his chest.
Look closely and you will see a
mime show, a subtle sleight of hand,
the restless dead initiating life.

At the Funeral of Pablo Neruda

The younger woman sees through
the picture frame with eyes that suggest
a black rage darker than her
grief. Her face is a poster
wanted by the police to post
in dark alleys defaced by guerrillas
who leave traces of their existence
in white paint and piss on, nights
the government enforcers are
working another part of town.
She is not screaming now
although her look proclaims:
this death is unjust and unnecessary
and someone must pay.
In this upside down world,
most likely it is she who will pay
strapped to an electronic torture
machine, hotwired from the brain
to the bowels, hung in suspended
animation in a prison of fear
from which no one, not even
the poet, escapes.
The older woman has already succumbed
to a grief, everyone here must know,
and she is seen crying without relief,
or shame. She has seen the present,
and, perhaps, knows the future as well.

The Three Burials of Pablo Neruda

First order of business, after the coup,
is all the opposition politicians are
to be collected and, no questions asked,
summarily shot. Then the journalists are
rounded up, the educators, the poets,
the musicians.

A man like Pablo, revered by all, is more
than an inconvenience, more than a nuisance,
but a threat, to be eliminated, less than two
weeks after previous regime's end, and
buried as quickly, and as anonymously,
as circumstances allow.

Pablo dead, the official releases say, of prostate
cancer, which conveniently flared up, and proved
fatal, before Pablo could formulate a response
to circumstantial changes in government.

Still, 40 years later, on the eve of his third
burial, at his intended resting place on Isla Negra,
his chauffer tells of a so-called doctor's
visit, of a hypodermic needle applied to the poet's
stomach, and the pain thereafter, horrible to behold;
the death throes, eternal dreaming in a minor key.

A quicker death, no doubt, than the suffering
endured by all the marked men, those poets,
musicians, philosophers, taken for final rides
in blue Falcon death squad cars to soccer stadium
for torture, humiliation, and murder. Pablo was
spared this; two exhumations don't count.
A kindness, no?

About the Author

Alan Catlin is retired from a long career in his unchosen profession in the "hospitality industry."

He has published well over sixty chapbooks and full-length books of poetry and prose. Most recently his fictional memoir/novel *Chaos Management* was published by Alien Buddha and is available on Amazon, as are many of his recent publications on a wide variety of subjects from art, to bar wars, to self-portraits that aren't self-portraits, to a series of book length memories which aren't "memories" per se, among many others. He won the 2017 Slipstream Chapbook Award for *Blue Velvet,* the first of eleven chapbooks channeling noir movies. Two of his books were named Most Neglected Books of the Year by the late Marvin Malone, editor of the legendary *Wormwood Review.*

www.ingramcontent.com/pod-product-compliance
Lightning Source LLC
LaVergne TN
LVHW011414080426
835511LV00005B/543